1 E

BOOK

David Atherton

Illustrated by
Harry Woodgate

WALKER BOOKS

For Sam, your mum is the best editor

D.A.

To Mum and Nanny, for sharing with me a love of baking,
and for all the wonderful cakes and memories

H.W.

First published 2022 by Walker Books Ltd, 87 Vauxhall Walk, London SE11 5HJ
10 9 8 7 6 5 4 3 2 1
Text © 2022 Nomadbaker Ltd   Illustrations © 2022 Harry Woodgate
The Great British Bake Off Baker logo™ is licensed by Love Productions Ltd
The right of David Atherton and Harry Woodgate to be identified as author and
illustrator respectively of this work has been asserted in accordance
with the Copyright, Designs and Patents Act 1988
This book has been typeset in Alice and Mrs Ant   Printed in China
British Library Cataloguing in Publication Data: a catalogue record for this book
is available from the British Library
ISBN 978-1-5295-0550-4   www.walker.co.uk

All recipes are for informational and/or entertainment purposes only;
please check all ingredients carefully if you have any allergies, and, if in doubt,
consult a health professional. Adult supervision is required for all recipes.

Introduction

For me and for lots of people, baking is the BEST! Everyone should learn how to bake. It's fun, it helps you relax *and* you feel good because you create something and learn something new every time you bake. I love playing music and dancing around the kitchen when I'm baking, and I hope your baking space becomes your happy place.

In this book you'll discover recipes for cakes, delicious breads, biscuits and pastries as well as yummy treats to enjoy with your friends and family. Whether you want bread rolls for your lunch, pies for a picnic, biscuits for afternoon tea, or even a fancy showstopper cake, this baking book has the recipe, whatever the occasion.

Baking isn't about making the perfect bakes; it's about having fun, trying new things and spending time together. Kneading bread, cutting out biscuits or icing a cake all need practice and concentration, but with a little perseverance, and some help from your family, you'll soon perfect your baking skills.

So, together with friends and family, pick a recipe from this book, tie on your apron and have fun!

David

Contents

Breads

Cakes

Sweet biscuits and bites

Pastries

Showstoppers

The art of baking

Baking is so much fun and I'm especially interested in the science behind it. If you want your cakes to rise, your bread to be soft or your biscuits to snap, then you need to follow the recipe carefully! Here are a few handy tips, tricks and facts to get your baking down to a fine art.

Raise your cake game

In order to rise, cakes need a raising agent like baking powder, which contains bicarbonate of soda (an alkali) and cream of tartar (an acid). When the powder gets wet, the alkali reacts with the acid to make tiny bubbles, helping the cake to rise and giving it a light, spongy texture.

Liven up your bread

Yeast is added to dough to make it rise. When combined with water, bread flour and salt, and left to prove (or rest) in a warm place, the yeast produces a gas that gets trapped in the dough, helping it to rise into a loaf of bread.

Spring into action!

Gluten is like little springs that add elasticity to bread dough. Yeast helps bread rise, but if there isn't enough gluten, your bread will fall flat. Gluten needs to be stretched out to work best, which is why you knead dough and stretch it with your hands.

Cold and crumbly

We want pastry to be crumbly, not chewy, and the best way to ensure this is to use cold butter. If you rub cold butter into flour, it coats the tiny bits of flour, stopping liquid from sticking the flour together, which would make the pastry stretchy and chewy.

Sweet and snappy

Sugar makes a biscuit snap! It melts when baking, then recrystallizes when cooling, which gives the biscuit its crunch. This is why biscuits are soft when they come out of the oven, but harden as they cool. If your biscuits are too soft, try leaving them in the oven for two more minutes.

Chill before baking

Because biscuits contain fat, which melts during cooking, biscuits spread out before they set into shape when fully cooked. If you chill the biscuit dough after you've cut out your shapes, they will take longer to melt in the oven, and won't spread out as much.

Before you get going

- It takes time to learn how to be safe in the kitchen. All the recipes in this book will need adult supervision – work together and have fun!

- If you have food allergies, or are cooking for someone, you need to check the ingredients list carefully.

- Finally, I am a nurse, so it is especially important for me to remind you to wash and dry your hands before cooking.

Store cupboard

 Yeast is dried and becomes alive once wet. In this book, we use fast-action yeast. You can use fresh yeast, but you'll need to double the weight. Always make sure yeast is in date.

 **Seeds** add a fun texture to your bakes, but also make them healthy. You can add a teaspoon of small seeds (such as poppy seeds or sesame seeds) to almost all types of bread, cakes, biscuits or pastries without having to change the recipe.

 Dried fruits add sweetness to a bake, but they're also full of vitamins, minerals and fibre, which are so good for us. It is easy to add dried fruit to bread and biscuits, but, with cakes, it is best to follow a recipe that includes them in the ingredients, otherwise the weight of the fruit could make your cake collapse.

 **Food colouring** is a great way to make a plain bake really special. I recommend using colour gels or pastes as they don't change the consistency of your mix. Look out for natural food colours that are made from vegetables and fruits, and don't use artificial chemicals.

 **Root vegetables** like carrots, parsnips or sweet potatoes make breads and cakes soft, sweet and, most importantly, healthy. You can experiment and switch parsnips for carrots, or sweet potato for swede.

 **Butter and spreads** are used in a lot of cakes, pastries and biscuits. Some bakes are known for their buttery flavour but there are lots of really good alternatives made with sunflower oil, soya beans or vegetable fats.

 Milks and yogurts were traditionally made with cow's milk. Nowadays you can buy all kinds of milks and yogurts made from plants, like oat milk, or soya yogurt. For the recipes in this book, you can use whichever milks, yogurts or spreads you like.

Weighing and measuring

- All recipes are measured in grams (g) and millilitres (ml).

- Tsp = teaspoon. Tbsp = tablespoon.

- The oven temperatures are in degrees Celsius (°C).

- Increase the temperature by 20°C for a non fan-assisted oven.

- Standard cupcake cases are the size in-between muffin cases and fairy cake cases.

Equipment list

Before you begin a recipe, it's a good idea to check what other equipment you might need. Here is a list of the equipment you will use in this book:

Baking paper

Baking tins

Baking trays

Beeswax wrap

Biscuit cutters

Bread scraper

Cake tins

Child's safety knife

Cooling rack

Digital weighing scales

Food processor

Frying pan (non-stick)

Grater

Large mixing bowl

Measuring jug

Measuring spoons

Muffin tray (12-hole)

Oven gloves

Oven timer

Pastry brush

Piping bag & nozzles

Pretty plates & bowls for serving

Rolling pin

Saucepan

Spatula

Standard cupcake cases

Stick blender

Tea towel

Remember to always ask an adult to help when you're baking.

BREADS

Ingredients

300g strong white
    bread flour, plus
    extra for dusting
50g strong brown
    bread flour
1 tsp fast-action yeast
½ tsp table salt
200ml warm water
1 medium egg

*Makes 8
braided buns*

Bread braids

Sometimes I like to make simple bread rolls and other times I like to be a little more fancy and braid the bread. These pretty bakes take more time, but look so beautiful and professional. Once baked, slice your bread braids in half and spread with any filling you like!

Method

1 Mix together the flours, yeast, salt and water in a mixing bowl until a sticky dough forms. Cover and leave for 10 minutes.

2 Knead the dough on a lightly floured surface for 5 minutes (do not add flour; it doesn't matter if it starts off sticky).

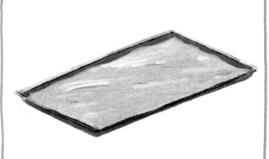

3 Cover and leave in a warm place until it doubles in size (this may take more than an hour).

4 Line a large baking tray with baking paper.

5 Knead the dough for 20 seconds, then divide it into 8 pieces.

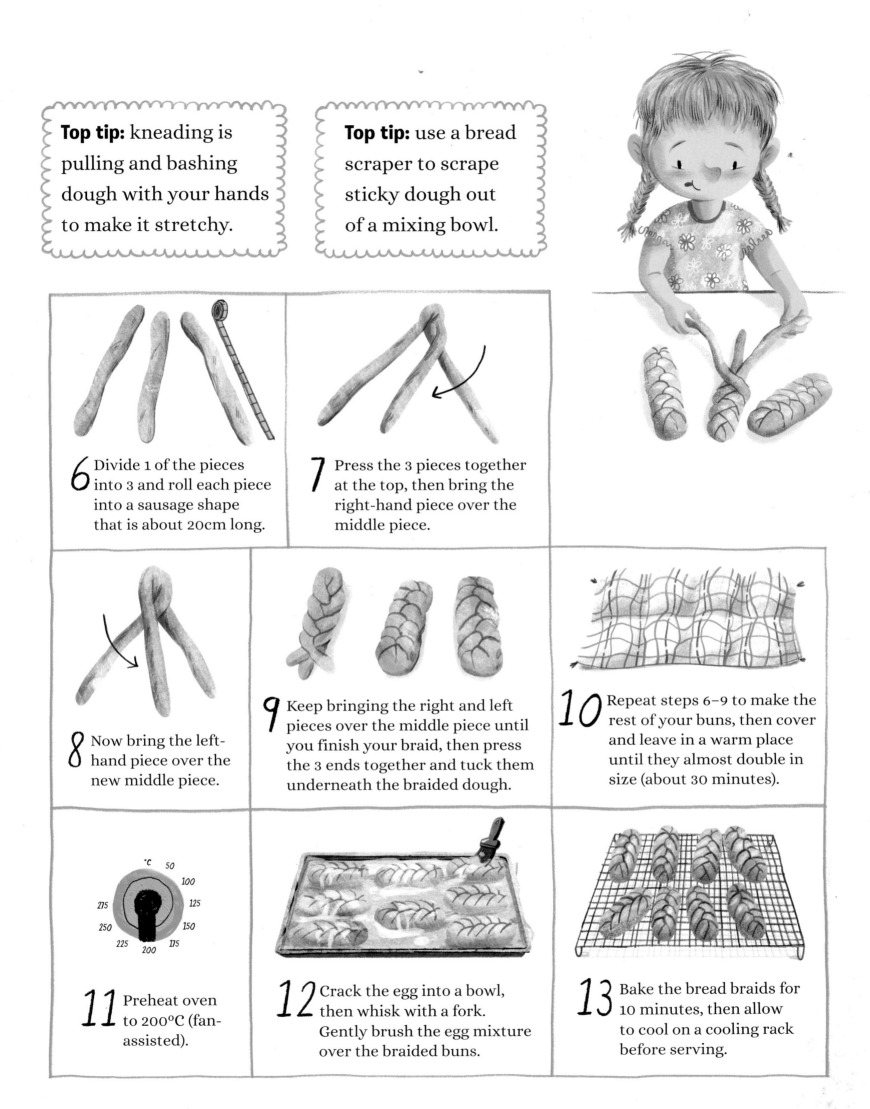

Top tip: kneading is pulling and bashing dough with your hands to make it stretchy.

Top tip: use a bread scraper to scrape sticky dough out of a mixing bowl.

6 Divide 1 of the pieces into 3 and roll each piece into a sausage shape that is about 20cm long.

7 Press the 3 pieces together at the top, then bring the right-hand piece over the middle piece.

8 Now bring the left-hand piece over the new middle piece.

9 Keep bringing the right and left pieces over the middle piece until you finish your braid, then press the 3 ends together and tuck them underneath the braided dough.

10 Repeat steps 6–9 to make the rest of your buns, then cover and leave in a warm place until they almost double in size (about 30 minutes).

11 Preheat oven to 200°C (fan-assisted).

12 Crack the egg into a bowl, then whisk with a fork. Gently brush the egg mixture over the braided buns.

13 Bake the bread braids for 10 minutes, then allow to cool on a cooling rack before serving.

Ingredients

300g strong white
bread flour, plus extra
for dusting

120ml boiling water

30g strong wholemeal
bread flour

1 tsp fast-action yeast

½ tsp table salt

110ml warm water

100g dark chocolate chips
(or a block of chocolate,
roughly chopped into
small pieces)

Makes 8 buns

Chocolate chip buns

I love trying baking techniques from other countries. This recipe uses a very special method called *Yudane*, which is from Japan. All you do is add boiling water to flour, right at the start of the recipe, which helps turn the bread super soft when baked. It takes time to make these sweet and gooey buns, so go and play while you're waiting for your dough to rise.

Method

1 Line a large baking tray with baking paper.

2 Weigh out 100g of white bread flour into a mixing bowl and pour in the boiling water. Mix to make a paste, then cover with a damp cloth and leave for 1 hour.

3 In another mixing bowl, add the rest of the white bread flour, all of the wholemeal flour, yeast, salt and warm water. Then, add your paste mixture to the bowl.

4 Stir together until a sticky dough forms, then cover and leave for 10 minutes.

5 Tip the dough out onto a lightly floured surface and sprinkle on the chocolate chips. Knead the dough for 3 minutes (do not add flour; it doesn't matter if it starts off sticky).

6 Leave covered in a warm spot until it doubles in size (this may take up to an hour).

7 Divide the dough into 8 pieces and roll each piece into a ball shape.

8 Cover and leave in a warm place for 30 minutes.

9 Preheat oven to 200°C (fan-assisted).

10 Bake the rolls for 15 minutes until golden at the edges, then leave to cool on a cooling rack before serving.

Top tip: sticky dough rises well and makes your bread really soft when baked.

Crunchy critter breadsticks

Why make boring breadsticks when you can make crispy and crunchy critter breadsticks? I've made a simple stick insect with this recipe, but I hope that you get creative and make all kinds of bugs and critters. The more legs, the better! Once your critter breadsticks have cooled, dip them in some hummus and enjoy!

Ingredients

170ml semi-skimmed milk

250g strong white bread flour, plus extra for dusting

50g strong brown bread flour

1 tsp fast-action yeast

1 tsp table salt

100g Cheddar cheese (grated)

30g coarse cornmeal (or polenta)

24 currants, for decoration

Makes 12 breadsticks

Method

1 Gently warm the milk in the microwave or in a small saucepan, over a low heat, until it is a little warm, but not too hot.

2 In a large mixing bowl, add the flours, yeast, salt and cheese. Pour in the milk and mix together until a dough forms. Cover and leave for 10 minutes.

3 Knead the dough on a lightly floured surface for 5 minutes (do not add flour; it doesn't matter if it starts off sticky).

4 Cover and leave in a warm place until it doubles in size (this usually takes about an hour).

5 Line 2 baking trays with baking paper.

6 Preheat oven to 170°C (fan-assisted).

7 Knock the air out of the dough, then divide into 12 golf-ball-sized pieces.

8 Roll each piece out into a sausage shape that is about 15cm long.

9 Sprinkle the cornmeal onto a plate and gently roll each piece in this (you're not looking for it to be completely coated).

10 Cut the sausage-shaped piece of dough into 2 pieces so that you have a long piece (for the body) and a short piece (for the legs).

11 Take the short piece of dough and make lots of little legs (you can cut the dough with scissors). Shape the long piece into a body then stick the legs onto it.

12 Make the rest of your insects and place them on the baking trays. For the eyes, push 2 currants, quite hard, into the dough of each critter.

13 Bake the critters for 20–25 minutes until they are nice and crunchy and golden. Yum!

Ingredients

Dough:

300g plain flour
½ tsp caster sugar
½ tsp table salt
1 tsp baking powder
250g live natural yogurt

Filling:

1 medium egg
200g feta cheese

Makes 10 rolls

Top tip: add chopped herbs to make the cheesy filling even tastier.

Top tip: brush the breads with a little beaten egg (at step 10) to give them a shiny finish when baked.

Filled soda breads

These filled rolls are so easy to make, but taste absolutely delicious! As the rolls are already filled, they are perfect for picnics and lunches on the go. You can use different types of cheese for the filling, but try to make sure the rolls are well sealed to stop the filling leaking out when baking.

Method

1 Toss the flour, sugar, salt and baking powder together in a mixing bowl. Add the yogurt and mix the ingredients together to make a sticky dough.

2 Cover and leave to rise for 30 minutes.

3 Line 2 baking trays with baking paper.

4 Break the egg into a bowl, beat with a fork, then crumble in the cheese and mix it all together.

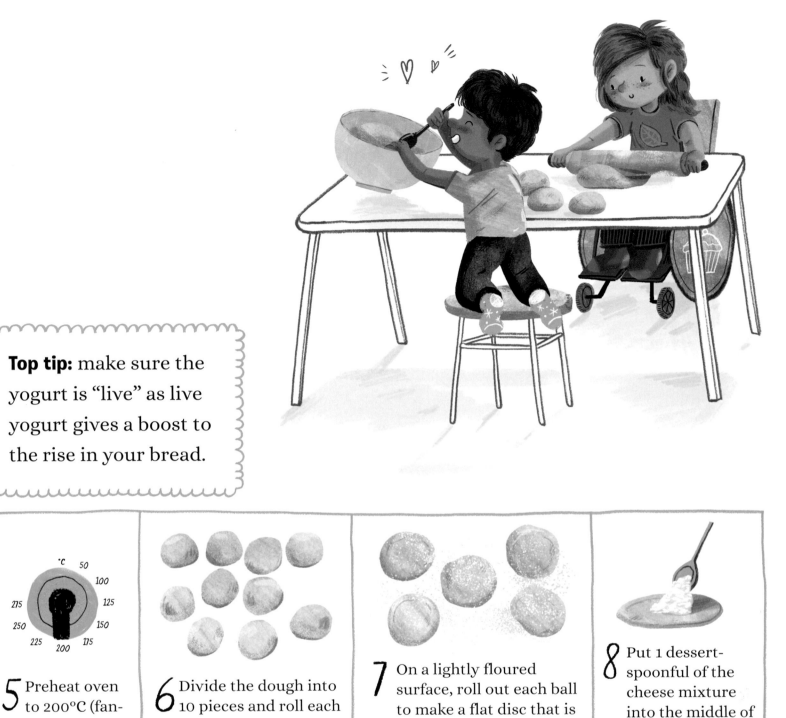

Top tip: make sure the yogurt is "live" as live yogurt gives a boost to the rise in your bread.

5 Preheat oven to 200°C (fan-assisted).

6 Divide the dough into 10 pieces and roll each piece into a ball.

7 On a lightly floured surface, roll out each ball to make a flat disc that is about 8–10cm wide.

8 Put 1 dessert-spoonful of the cheese mixture into the middle of one of the discs.

9 Pull the edges of the dough around the filling and pinch them closed where they meet. Turn the roll over.

10 Gently roll the filled bread until it is about 8–10cm wide again, then set aside on the baking tray while you make the others.

11 Bake for 10–12 minutes until golden, and once out of the oven, leave to cool a little. Best eaten still slightly warm.

Hot cross hedgehogs

These bread buns are shiny, golden and sticky. The hedgehog spikes go really crunchy when baked, but the bun underneath stays soft and springy. You can use whatever dried fruit you like. I didn't like mixed peel as a child, but love it now. If you're eating the hot cross hedgehogs the day after baking, it's best to slice them in half, toast and spread with butter.

Ingredients

280g warm water

40g soft, pitted prunes

300g strong white
    bread flour

180g strong wholemeal
    bread flour

2 tsp fast-action yeast

1 tsp table salt

1 tsp ground mixed spice

80g raisins, plus extra
    for decoration

50g chopped mixed peel

1 medium egg

9 tsp runny honey,
    to glaze

Method

1 Pour the warm water into a jug. Add the prunes and whizz with a stick blender until the prunes have been liquidized (or until there are very little bits of prune left).

2 In a mixing bowl, add the flours, yeast, salt, spice and prune water. Mix with a spatula until a dough forms. Cover and leave for 10 minutes.

Makes 9 buns

3 Add the raisins and mixed peel and knead for 2 minutes (do not add flour; it doesn't matter if it starts off sticky).

4 Cover and leave in a warm place until it doubles in size (this may take more than an hour).

5 Divide the dough into 9 pieces and roll into balls.

6 Gently pinch one end of each ball to make a snout shape.

7 Line a large baking tray with baking paper and place each hedgehog onto the baking tray (keep at least 3cm between each bun).

8 Cover and leave to rise for 30 minutes.

9 Preheat oven to 200°C (fan-assisted).

10 Break the egg into a small bowl, whisk with a fork and brush each bun with the egg mixture.

11 Snip the dough with scissors to make little spines. Add raisins for the eyes and a single raisin for the nose, pushing them down quite hard into the dough.

12 Bake for 12 minutes, then allow to cool.

13 Glaze by brushing honey on the buns when cooled, but still a little warm.

Ingredients

Dough:

150ml semi-skimmed milk

60ml boiling water

150g strong white
   bread flour, plus extra
   for dusting

50g strong brown
   bread flour

150g plain flour

1 tsp fast-action yeast

1 tsp soft brown sugar

1 tsp table salt

Water bath:

1 litre of water

2 tsp bicarbonate of soda

Topping:

20g butter

50g caster sugar

1 tsp ground cinnamon

Makes 10 pretzels

Cinnamon pretzel letters

Pretzels are made from soft dough that is usually curled round into twisty shapes. In this recipe, you can twist the dough into any letter shape you'd like. I like to make my initials, "D" and "A", but you can spell out your whole name. The dough is then poached in simmering water before baking, which gives the pretzels a delicious chewy texture. Yum!

Method

1 Line 2 baking trays with baking paper and set aside.

2 Pour the milk and boiling water into a jug and stir.

3 Add the flours, yeast, sugar and salt into a large mixing bowl. Pour in the milk-water and mix together until a sticky dough forms. Cover and leave for 10 minutes.

4 Knead the dough on a lightly floured surface for 5 minutes (do not add flour; it doesn't matter if it starts off sticky).

5 Cover and leave in a warm place until it doubles in size (this may take up to an hour).

6 Cut out 10 squares (about 15cm x 15cm) of baking paper.

7 Preheat oven to 200°C (fan-assisted).

8 Divide the dough into 10 pieces and roll into sausage shapes.

9 Make each sausage shape into a letter shape (you can use scissors to cut the dough into sections). Place each letter onto a baking paper square.

10 Bring a large saucepan of 1 litre of water to the boil, then reduce the heat to a simmer and sprinkle in the bicarbonate of soda.

11 Ask an adult to gently tip each pretzel off the baking paper square and into the water. You can fit about 3 letters in at a time.

12 Poach for 1 minute, then remove with a slotted spoon and transfer to the lined baking trays. Once the trays are full, bake for 8 minutes until golden brown.

13 Melt the butter in the microwave or a small saucepan. Toss together the sugar and cinnamon in a small bowl.

14 Transfer the pretzels to a cooling rack. When the pretzels are still a little warm, brush with the melted butter and sprinkle the cinnamon sugar on top.

Top tip: poach means to cook something in gently bubbling, boiling water. Always make sure an adult is on hand to help with tricky steps like step 11!

23

Savoury scone volcanoes

These scones are quick to make and so yummy to eat. For this recipe, you stack different-sized scones on top of each other and push a piece of cheese into the middle. While the scones are baking, the cheese erupts, like lava from a volcano! Just make sure that the "lava" has cooled down before tucking in!

Ingredients

350g self-raising flour,
    plus extra for dusting
1 tsp baking powder
1 tsp smoked paprika
80g unsalted butter
    (diced into 1cm cubes)
165ml semi-skimmed
    milk, plus extra for
    brushing
1 tsp lemon juice
200g Red Leicester (100g
    grated, 100g sliced
    into 10 small, finger-
    sized batons)

Makes 8-10 stacked scones

Method

1 Preheat oven to 200°C (fan-assisted).

2 Line a baking tray with baking paper.

3 Put the flour, baking powder, paprika and butter into a mixing bowl. Rub with your fingers until the mixture looks like breadcrumbs.

4 Pour the milk and lemon juice into the mixing bowl. Sprinkle in the grated cheese and bring the ingredients together to make a dough.

5 Tip the dough onto a lightly floured surface and roll it out until it is 1cm thick. Cut out 3 scones using a 7cm, 6cm and 5cm cutter.

6 Brush the tops of the scones with milk, then transfer the largest scone to the lined baking tray. Stack the other 2 scones on top, with the smallest added last.

7 Make the rest of the scone towers, then gently push a baton of cheese into the middle of each tower (don't poke it in too far – you want to see the lava flowing out).

8 Bake for 12–14 minutes, until nicely golden. Allow to cool on a cooling rack. Eat while they are still a little warm.

CAKES

Lemon drizzle cake

This is a classic cake and lots of people have a special family recipe. In my family, we like to make sure it is very zingy, so we add lots of lemon to the topping. If you like it sweeter, you can use orange juice instead of lemon, and if you like it really zingy, then try using limes. However you like it, this moist and light cake is sure to be a firm favourite!

Method

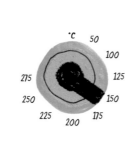

1 Preheat oven to 160°C (fan-assisted).

2 Put the oats into a blender and blitz until you have a rough powder.

3 Line the bottom of a 20cm loaf tin with baking paper and grease the sides with a little butter.

4 Add the sugar, butter and oil to a large mixing bowl and beat together with an electric mixer until light and pale.

Ingredients

Cake:

60g porridge oats

160g caster sugar

90g unsalted butter
   (at room temperature),
   plus extra for greasing

80ml vegetable oil

Zest of 2 lemons

3 medium eggs

190g plain flour

1 ½ tsp baking
   powder

Topping:

75g caster sugar, plus
   extra for sprinkling

50ml lemon juice (from
   2 lemons above)

Makes 10-12 slices

5 Zest the lemons with a fine grater and add this to the mixture.

6 Crack 1 egg into the bowl and beat until combined. Add the second egg. Beat it into the mixture, then add the third egg and beat again until combined.

7 Add the flour, oats and baking powder and mix with a spatula.

8 Pour into the tin and bake for 50–60 minutes (or until a skewer comes out clean).

Top tip: add lemon peel to the top of the cake to make it look pretty and give it an extra zingy taste!

9 While the cake is still warm, put the sugar and lemon juice for the topping into a small saucepan and heat until the sugar has just dissolved.

10 Use a skewer to poke about 20 deep holes into the warm cake, then spoon over the drizzle topping and sprinkle a little extra sugar on top.

11 Remove from the tin when cool and serve.

Cheeky mouse cakes

Some people are scared of mice, but I think they're really cute. This cupcake recipe uses piped buttercream to make a little mouse face, with a pointy nose. Don't worry if you don't get the hang of piping the icing straight away. Take your time, practise lots and you'll get there!

Ingredients

Cakes:

65g caster sugar

65g soft brown sugar

100ml vegetable oil

1 tsp vanilla extract

2 medium eggs

100g swede

120g plain flour

1 ½ tsp baking powder

1 tsp ground mixed spice

1 tsp ground cinnamon

Topping:

75g unsalted butter
    (at room temperature)

150g icing sugar, plus
    extra for dusting

1 tsp vanilla extract

24 white chocolate
    buttons

24 currants

12 little ball-shaped
    sweets (or sprinkles)

12 strawberry laces

Makes 12 cupcakes

Method

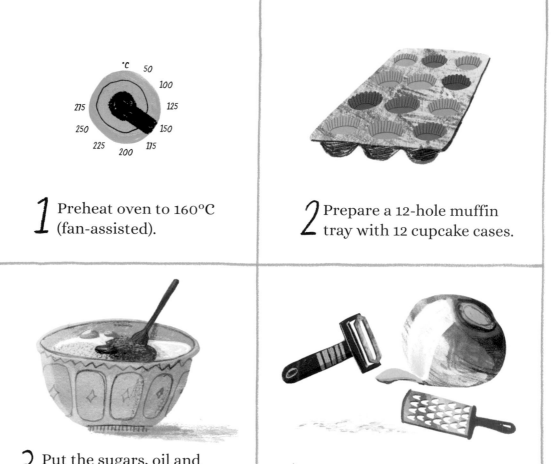

1 Preheat oven to 160°C (fan-assisted).

2 Prepare a 12-hole muffin tray with 12 cupcake cases.

3 Put the sugars, oil and vanilla into a mixing bowl. Crack in the 2 eggs and beat until smooth.

4 Peel and finely grate the swede until you have 100g. Add the grated swede to the mixture.

5 Add the flour, baking powder and spices, then stir until you have a smooth batter.

6 Use a dessertspoon to fill the cupcake cases three-quarters full.

7 Bake for 25 minutes. Allow to cool in the tin for 5 minutes, then remove from the tray and leave to cool completely on a cooling rack.

8 Put the butter, icing sugar and vanilla into a mixing bowl and beat until smooth (you can add 1 tsp of warm water to help loosen the mixture).

9 Put the buttercream into a piping bag fitted with a small swirly nozzle (or use a sandwich bag and cut off the corner when you are ready to pipe).

10 Pipe a swirl of buttercream in the middle of the cupcake and try to make it come up to a point (this will be the mouse's nose).

11 Using a small sieve, dust with icing sugar.

12 Gently press 2 chocolate buttons in for the ears, add 2 currants for the eyes, a little ball-shaped sweetie for the nose and a strawberry lace for the tail.

13 Repeat steps 10–12 until you have 12 cheeky mouse cakes!

Ingredients

A little butter, for greasing
2 large eggs
50g caster sugar
50g self-raising flour
½ tsp baking powder
100g strawberry jam
100g plain Greek yogurt
2 tsp icing sugar, for dusting

Makes 10 servings

Jam Swiss roll

Most cakes come in layers, but a Swiss roll comes rolled up. This is a tricky bake to get perfect, but when you do, it is a cake that is sure to impress! The sponge is light and fluffy and there's a delicious fruity filling inside.

Serving suggestion: add some sparkle to your Swiss roll by sprinkling a little edible glitter over the rolled-up cake.

Method

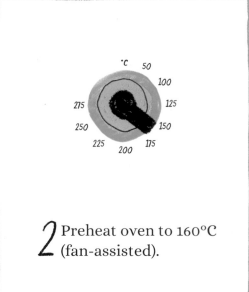

1 Line the base of a baking tray that is 30cm x 20cm (and 2cm deep) with baking paper, and grease the edges of the tray with a little butter.

2 Preheat oven to 160°C (fan-assisted).

3 Break the eggs into a large mixing bowl. Add the sugar, then whisk together with an electric mixer until thick and pale.

4 Test that the mixture is the right consistency by lifting the whisk up and gently shaking it back and forth over the bowl. This should leave a trail of batter that doesn't sink back into the mixture.

5 Sift the self-raising flour and baking powder into the mixture and gently fold in with the spatula.

6 Pour the mixture onto the baking tray and gently smooth down with a spatula until it is roughly level and fills the tray. Bake for 10 minutes.

7 Ask an adult to turn the cake out onto a clean tea towel. Roll the sponge up with the towel wrapped inside it and cool.

8 Gently unroll the cake and remove the tea towel. Peel off the baking paper. Spread with the jam, then dollop on the yogurt and smooth it down.

9 Gently roll the cake back up, transfer to a plate or serving board and dust with icing sugar, using a sieve.

Chocolate garden cups

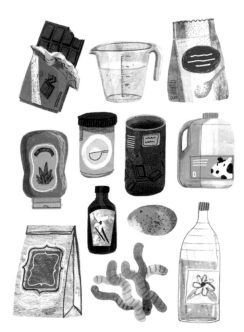

When I was a kid, I loved making mud pies in the garden. This inspired my chocolatey garden cups recipe, made with chocolate-sauce mud, crumbly cake soil and gummy worms! This pudding is assembled in 8 teacups and is perfect for a party. Serve on a saucer with a teaspoon on the side and see how long it takes your friends and family to find a worm in the chocolate mud!

Serving suggestion: you can serve the sauce cold, or warm it up a little before you pour it over the cake.

Ingredients

Chocolate sauce:

25g milk chocolate

100ml water

50g caster sugar

40g agave syrup

2 tbsp cocoa powder

Cake:

170g plain flour

25g cocoa powder

250g caster sugar

1 ½ tsp baking powder

90ml semi-skimmed milk

70ml vegetable oil, plus extra for greasing

1 large egg

2 tsp vanilla extract

150ml water

Decoration:

16 gummy worms

Makes 8 servings

Method

1 Start with the chocolate sauce. Break the chocolate into small pieces (or blitz it in a food processor) and set aside.

2 Put all the other sauce ingredients into a small saucepan. Heat over a medium heat and stir until simmering.

3 Take off the heat and beat in the chocolate, then leave to cool.

4 Grease a 20cm baking tin with a little oil and line with baking paper.

5 Preheat oven to 170°C (fan-assisted).

36

6 Toss the flour, cocoa powder, sugar and baking powder together in a mixing bowl.

7 Add the rest of the cake ingredients to the bowl and beat everything together until smooth.

8 Pour into the tin and bake for 30 minutes, then allow to cool completely on a cooling rack.

9 Measure the width of the teacup. Turn the cake out and cut 8 discs using a cutter that is about the same size as the width of your teacup.

10 Gather the cake offcuts and crumble them with your fingers until they look like breadcrumbs.

11 Gently push a disc of cake down to the bottom of each teacup. Pour over the chocolate sauce until all of the teacups are about two-thirds full.

12 Sprinkle the cake crumbs on top of the sauce, then add a couple of gummy worms to each cup so that they hang over the side.

13 Serve your chocolate garden cups on a teacup saucer with a teaspoon on the side. Yum!

Rainbow butterfly cake

This beautiful cake has all the colours of the rainbow! You can decorate it however you like, but remember, butterfly wings are symmetrical, which means that the shape and pattern is the same on each side. This cake uses ingredients that are suitable for a vegan, and tastes light, fluffy and delicious. It's the perfect celebration cake for a friend coming round for tea.

Ingredients

Cake:

220g plain flour

210g caster sugar

1 ½ tsp baking powder

¼ tsp of table salt

1 tsp white malt vinegar

200ml water

70ml vegetable oil

2 tsp vegan yellow food
   colouring

Topping:

300g icing sugar

40g soya spread (or
   sunflower spread), plus
   extra for greasing

25ml oat milk

1 tsp vegan red food
   colouring

1 tsp vanilla extract

Rainbow-coloured vegan
   sweets, to decorate

Makes 12 servings

Method

1 Preheat oven to 180°C (fan-assisted).

2 Line the bottom of a 23cm round cake tin with baking paper and grease the sides with a little spread.

3 Put all the cake ingredients into a mixing bowl and beat until smooth.

4 Pour into the prepared tin and bake for 30 minutes.

5 Allow to cool for 5 minutes in the tin, then turn the cake out onto a cooling rack to cool completely.

6 Put the icing sugar in a mixing bowl with the spread, half the milk, food colouring and vanilla. Mix with an electric whisk (or stick blender) until smooth and very thick.

7 Gradually add the rest of the milk, beating the mixture with the electric whisk until smooth and soft.

8 Cut the cake in half, then cut out a small triangle shape from the long edge of both cake halves and set aside.

9 Flip the cakes around, so that their circular edges are touching. They should look like butterfly wings.

10 Spread the icing all over the wings, then gently push the triangle-shaped pieces of cake onto the centre of the wings to make the butterfly body.

11 Decorate the iced wings with your sweets. Remember, the pattern should match on both sides.

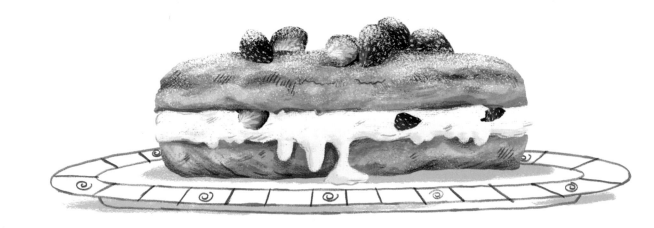

Ingredients

Cake:

50g unsalted butter
   (at room temperature)

60g live natural yogurt

85g caster sugar

1 large egg

1 tsp vanilla extract

110g plain flour

1 tsp baking powder

Filling & topping:

300g vanilla ice cream

300g strawberries
   (sliced)

1 tbsp icing sugar,
   for dusting

> Makes 8-10 servings <

Ice-cream sandwich cake

Sometimes we have cake and sometimes we have ice cream, so why not have BOTH? This ice-cream cake will look beautiful served as a dessert after a special dinner and you can choose your favourite ice-cream flavour for the middle, or even do a combination. Delicious!

Method

1 Preheat oven to 180°C (fan-assisted).

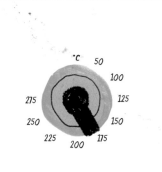

2 Cut a piece of baking paper that is about 40cm x 30cm. Scrunch it into a ball, then open it out and push into a 20cm loaf tin.

3 Cream together the butter, yogurt and sugar until pale and creamy.

4 Break the egg and beat it in with the vanilla (don't worry if it looks curdled). Add the flour and baking powder and stir until just mixed.

5 Transfer to the tin and bake for 20–25 minutes (or until a skewer comes out clean).

6 Allow to cool for 5 minutes, then remove from the tin and allow to cool completely.

7 Remove the ice cream from the freezer and allow to soften (for at least 15 minutes).

8 Line the loaf tin with another 40cm x 30cm sheet of baking paper. Slice the cake in half (lengthways) and put the top half (top-side down) back into the bottom of the tin.

9 Spread the soft ice cream over the sponge, then layer three-quarters of the sliced strawberries on the ice cream.

10 Place the other half of the cake on top and push down gently.

11 Put into the freezer for at least 30 minutes (or longer, if needed).

12 Remove from the tin by tipping it upside down onto a plate, lifting up the tin and peeling back the paper.

13 Arrange the last of the sliced strawberries on top and dust heavily with icing sugar.

Ingredients

Cake:

2 Braeburn apples

3 medium eggs

2 tbsp honey

90ml vegetable oil

40g currants

120g plain flour

1 ½ tsp baking
   powder

2 tsp ground cinnamon

Glaze:

120g icing sugar

½ tsp ground cinnamon

2 tsp lemon juice

Makes 9 cupcakes

Autumn apple cakes

I grew up with apple trees in our garden, so we made lots of bakes using apples. These little cakes are so moist and tasty, but are healthy too. They're also the perfect size to take on a picnic as a sweet and fruity treat!

Method

1 Preheat oven to 180°C (fan-assisted) and prepare a muffin tin with 9 cupcake cases.

2 Peel the apples, then cut them into quarters and remove the cores (you will need help doing this).

3 Coarsely grate the apples into a mixing bowl until you have 200g of grated apple.

4 Add the eggs, honey, oil and currants and stir with a spatula until combined.

5 Add the flour, baking powder and cinnamon, and stir until you have a glossy mixture.

6 Use a tablespoon to fill the cupcake cases three-quarters full. Bake for 18–20 minutes until nicely golden, then cool on a cooling rack.

7 Mix the icing sugar, cinnamon and lemon juice in a small bowl. When the cakes are still a bit warm, spoon on the glaze.

Swampy banana choco cake

This is a kind of MAGIC cake. You make a cake mixture, then, when you pour boiling water on top, it moves through the cake, and ... *hey presto*, you have a thick chocolatey sauce at the bottom and moist chocolate cake on top! This sticky, swampy pudding is perfect to warm you up on a chilly day.

Ingredients

Cake:

150g self-raising flour

110g caster sugar

25g cocoa powder

1 medium egg

50g unsalted butter,
   plus extra for greasing

120ml semi-skimmed milk

1 tsp vanilla extract

1 ripe banana (peeled
   and cut into chunks)

Topping:

75g caster sugar

20g cocoa powder

250ml boiling water

Makes 6 servings

Method

1 Preheat oven to 160°C (fan-assisted).

2 Grease a 20cm square baking tin with a little butter.

3 In a mixing bowl, toss together the flour, caster sugar and cocoa powder.

4 Crack the egg into a small bowl then pour into a blender. Add the butter, milk, vanilla and banana chunks, then blend until smooth.

5 Pour into the flour mixture and stir everything together until combined. Transfer the batter to the tin.

6 For the topping, toss together the sugar and cocoa powder in a small bowl, then sprinkle onto the batter.

7 Ask an adult to carefully pour the boiling water over the topping and to transfer the very hot tin into the oven (using oven gloves).

8 Bake for 30 minutes, then allow to stand for 10 minutes before serving into bowls.

43

Ingredients

Cakes:

2 medium eggs

80g Greek yogurt

80ml light olive oil

120g caster sugar

120g plain flour

1 ½ tsp baking
   powder

2 tsp vanilla extract

50g blueberries

50g raspberries

Topping:

100g Greek yogurt

30g icing sugar, plus
   extra for dusting

25g blueberries

25g raspberries

Makes 12 cupcakes

Summer berry yogurt cakes

Berries and yogurt are a perfect summer flavour combination. Yogurt is also brilliant for giving cakes a bit more rise. Live yogurt has good bacteria inside that make acids. Cake mixture needs acid to rise in the oven, so adding yogurt means you're getting the extra boost for free!

Method

1 Preheat oven to 180°C (fan-assisted).

2 Prepare a 12-hole muffin tray with 12 cupcake cases.

3 Break the eggs into a mixing bowl, then add the yogurt, oil, sugar, flour, baking powder and vanilla and mix until smooth.

4 Stir through the fruit, then fill each case three-quarters full with the batter.

5 Bake for 20–25 minutes (or until a skewer comes out clean). Allow to cool on a cooling rack.

6 Gently mix the yogurt and icing sugar together in a small bowl.

7 Spoon a tablespoon of yogurt mix onto each cake, top with fruit and dust with icing sugar, using a sieve.

SWEET BISCUITS AND BITES

Sticky chocolate flapjacks

This very simple but delicious flapjack is packed full of goodness and energy. The key thing here is to use really soft dates, which go wonderfully sticky when blended and baked. This is my go-to sweet snack if I'm heading off on an adventure, hiking a mountain, rowing down a river or bouncing on a trampoline.

Ingredients

100g butter, plus extra
    for greasing
100g golden syrup
130g soft pitted dates
350g muesli
100g white chocolate

Makes 16 flapjacks

Method

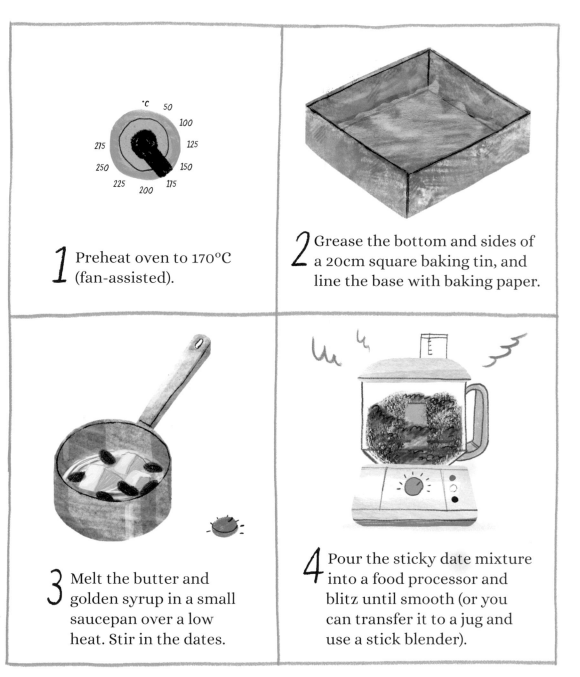

1 Preheat oven to 170°C (fan-assisted).

2 Grease the bottom and sides of a 20cm square baking tin, and line the base with baking paper.

3 Melt the butter and golden syrup in a small saucepan over a low heat. Stir in the dates.

4 Pour the sticky date mixture into a food processor and blitz until smooth (or you can transfer it to a jug and use a stick blender).

5 Add the muesli to a mixing bowl and pour in the sticky date mixture. Stir with a spatula until everything is well coated.

6 Tip into the tin and push down with the spatula until level.

7 Bake for 25 minutes until golden, then allow to cool in the tin.

8 Break the chocolate into a small heatproof bowl. Place the bowl over a small saucepan that has a little water in it. Bring the water to a simmer and stir the chocolate until it melts.

9 Using a tablespoon, drizzle or splatter the chocolate over the flapjack. I like to splatter it around!

10 Allow the chocolate to set (this takes 15 minutes in the fridge if you want to speed it up). Cut the flapjack into 16 squares, remove from the tin and serve.

Ingredients

70ml light olive oil, plus
  extra for greasing

170g caster sugar

2 tsp vanilla extract

170g plain flour

30g cocoa powder

1 tsp baking powder

¼ tsp table salt

200g courgette (finely
  grated)

35g milk chocolate chips

35g white chocolate chips

Makes 20 bite-sized
brownies

Chocolate brownie bites

Brownies should be squidgy, chocolatey, and you should always want "just one more". These brownies tick all the boxes, but are also a little healthier because they are made with courgettes, which make them extra soft and moist.

Top tip: you can use vegan chocolate if you want to make the recipe vegan.

Method

1 Preheat oven to 180°C (fan-assisted).

2 Put the oil, sugar, vanilla, flour, cocoa powder, baking powder and salt into a mixing bowl. Rub with your fingers until it looks like a crumble mix.

3 Add the grated courgette to the mixing bowl. Tip in the chocolate chips and gently stir until combined, then allow to sit for 5 minutes.

4 In the meantime, grease the bottom and sides of a 20cm square baking tin with a little olive oil, then line the tin with baking paper.

5 Stir the mixture again and pour into the tin.

6 Bake for 20 minutes. The middle should still be soft, but that is how we want it – nice and gooey in the centre and firmer on the edges.

7 Allow to cool before cutting into 20 bite-sized squares.

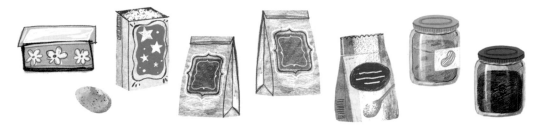

Ingredients

Biscuits:

150g unsalted butter (at room temperature)

50g smooth peanut butter

100g icing sugar

1 medium egg

200g plain flour, plus extra for dusting

50g wholemeal plain flour

2 tsp caster sugar, for sprinkling

Filling:

150g smooth peanut butter

150g strawberry jam

Makes 12 biscuits

PB and jammie biscuits

Peanut butter and jam on toast is the BEST!!! So, what could make jammie biscuits even better? Peanut butter, of course! I like strawberry jam, but you can use any flavour of jam or nut butter you prefer. You'll need a mini biscuit cutter to make the holes in these biscuits. I like to make star-shaped holes, but you can choose whichever shape you like. These fruity, nutty biscuits are a perfect afternoon treat.

Top tip: use beeswax wrap to wrap your dough.

Method

1 Add the butter to a large mixing bowl (make sure the butter is at room temperature and soft). Spoon in the peanut butter and icing sugar and beat everything together until smooth.

2 Crack the egg over a little bowl, then gently tip the white and yolk onto your open hand, letting the white fall through your fingers into the bowl. Drop the egg yolk into the large mixing bowl and beat it in.

3 Add the flours and mix with a spoon, then knead with your hands to make a dough.

4 Wrap the dough and chill in the fridge for 20 minutes.

5 Preheat oven to 160°C (fan-assisted).

6 On a lightly floured surface, roll out the dough until it is 0.5cm thick, then cut out 24 biscuits using an 8cm biscuit cutter.

7 Line 2 large baking trays with baking paper. Place 12 of the cut-out biscuits onto 1 of the baking trays and set aside.

8 Transfer the remaining 12 biscuits to the second baking tray. Cut a small hole out of each biscuit, using a mini biscuit cutter.

9 Brush the holey biscuits with the egg white, then lightly sprinkle with sugar.

10 Bake both trays of biscuits for 12–15 minutes until the edges are golden, then allow to cool for 5 minutes on the trays before transferring to a cooling rack.

11 When the biscuits have cooled, spread a small teaspoon of peanut butter onto each biscuit without a hole, then add a blob of jam in the middle.

12 Gently press a holey biscuit on top of each peanut-butter-and-jam biscuit to make 12 sandwiched biscuits.

Fruit crumble bars

Crumble is one of my favourite desserts, but to eat crumble you need a bowl and spoon (and maybe some custard too). These fruit crumble bites can be easily carried around, which means you can enjoy crumble wherever you go. Woohoo!

Ingredients

100g butter

75g peanut butter

140g plain flour

40g wholemeal flour

1 tsp ground cinnamon

1 tsp baking powder

100g caster sugar

80g soft brown sugar

130g porridge oats

50ml water

300g frozen raspberries
    (defrosted and drained)

1 heaped tbsp cornflour

2 tbsp runny honey

1 tbsp icing sugar, to dust

⇒ Makes 21 little bars ⇐

Method

1 Scrunch up a big piece of baking paper. Open it out then push it into a 25cm x 35cm baking tin, making sure it comes up the sides of the tin.

2 Preheat oven to 180°C (fan-assisted).

3 Put the butter, peanut butter, flours, cinnamon and baking powder into a food processor and blitz until the mixture resembles breadcrumbs.

4 Tip the mixture into a large mixing bowl.

Top tip: if you don't have a food processor for step 3, rub the ingredients together with your fingers.

5 Add the sugars, oats and water to the mixing bowl and rub with your fingers until it looks like a crumble mix.

6 Press three-quarters of this mixture into the tin to make the base of the bars and bake for 15 minutes.

7 Tip the frozen raspberries and cornflour into a bowl. Add the honey and stir together.

8 Once the base is out of the oven, spoon the raspberry mixture onto the base, then sprinkle the remaining crumble mixture on top.

9 Bake for 35 minutes, then allow to cool fully.

10 Ask an adult to lift out of the tin using the edges of the baking paper. Cut into 3 long rows, then cut each row into 7, so that you have 21 little bars.

11 Dust with icing sugar, using a sieve.

Ingredients

Biscuits:

80g unsalted butter

50g tinned sweetcorn
   (drained)

1 tsp vanilla extract

50 caster sugar

140g plain flour, plus
   extra for dusting

60g instant custard
   powder

Filling:

90g icing sugar

60g unsalted butter
   (room temperature)

1 tsp vanilla extract

Sweet custard creams

My favourite biscuits are custard creams and I love dipping
them into a cup of warm milk. Have you ever tried making
the biscuits you buy in the shops? It is actually very easy,
fun, and you can even make them a bit healthier. These
biscuits have sweetcorn in them, but taste of vanilla custard.

> Makes 18 biscuits <

Method

1 Line 2 large
baking trays
with baking
paper.

2 Put the butter, sweetcorn and
vanilla into a beaker and blitz
with a stick blender until smooth
(don't worry if the sweetcorn
doesn't completely blend into
the butter mixture).

3 In a mixing bowl, add the butter
mixture along with the sugar,
flour and custard powder and
mix with a spatula (or use your
hands) until a dough forms.

4 Cover and chill in the fridge for 30 minutes.

5 Preheat oven to 160°C (fan-assisted).

6 On a lightly floured surface, roll out the dough until it is 0.5cm thick.

7 Cut out 36 little biscuits using a 4cm biscuit cutter. Place 18 biscuits onto each lined baking tray.

8 Bake for 10 minutes until just golden at the edges.

9 While the biscuits are in the oven, mix all the filling ingredients until you have a thick, smooth buttercream (you may need to add 1 tsp of warm water to loosen the mixture).

10 Once the biscuits are cool, sandwich 2 biscuits together with a dollop of buttercream. Repeat until you have 18 custard creams.

Top tip: use a crimped, rectangular-shaped cutter to cut out your biscuit dough.

No-bake tiffin

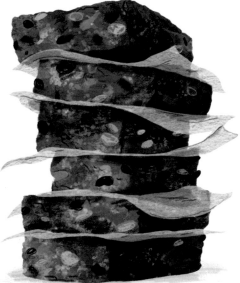

I've broken the rules here and added a recipe that doesn't need baking. Don't worry though, it still uses plenty of ingredients that you'll find in baking and has the added bonus of being quick and easy to make. Once this biscuity, chocolatey treat is set, cut it into chunks and enjoy.

Ingredients

150g digestive biscuits

100g unsalted roasted peanuts

100g raisins

150g dark chocolate

40g golden syrup

40g runny honey

60g unsalted butter, plus extra for greasing

50g peanut butter

Makes 25 bite-sized pieces

Method

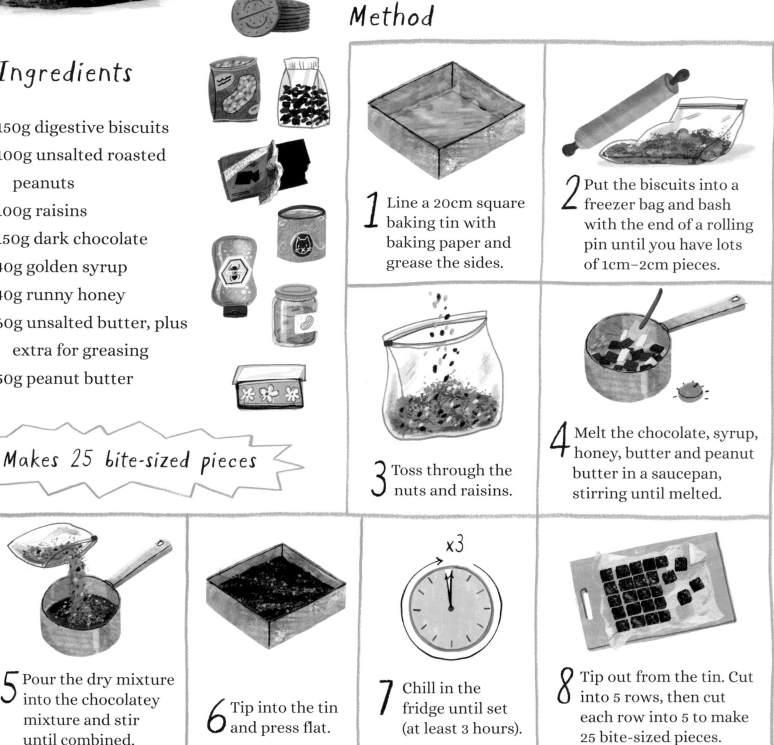

1 Line a 20cm square baking tin with baking paper and grease the sides.

2 Put the biscuits into a freezer bag and bash with the end of a rolling pin until you have lots of 1cm–2cm pieces.

3 Toss through the nuts and raisins.

4 Melt the chocolate, syrup, honey, butter and peanut butter in a saucepan, stirring until melted.

5 Pour the dry mixture into the chocolatey mixture and stir until combined.

6 Tip into the tin and press flat.

7 Chill in the fridge until set (at least 3 hours).

8 Tip out from the tin. Cut into 5 rows, then cut each row into 5 to make 25 bite-sized pieces.

PASTRIES

Ingredients

100g vermicelli rice
    noodles
300ml boiling water
    (or enough to cover
    the noodles)
1 medium carrot
¼ of a white cabbage
2 spring onions
1 garlic clove (minced)
1 tsp Chinese five spice
2 tbsp soy sauce
12 square sheets of
    spring roll wrappers
    (or filo pastry)
1 tbsp vegetable oil,
    for brushing

Makes 12 rolls

Baked spring rolls

These little crispy parcels are made all over Asia and are usually deep-fried. This version is baked, but the rolls still turn out very crispy. If you can't find spring roll wrappers, you can use sheets of filo pastry (cut into 12cm x 12cm squares). Once baked, leave the rolls to cool a little, then eat with your favourite dipping sauce. I love hoisin!

Method

1 Put the vermicelli noodles into a bowl, cover with boiling water and leave for 5 minutes. Drain and transfer to a large mixing bowl.

2 Peel and coarsely grate the carrot, then toss it in the mixing bowl with the noodles.

3 Chop the cabbage and spring onions as finely as you can and add to the bowl.

4 Add the garlic, Chinese five spice and soy sauce and toss around for a minute, using 2 forks.

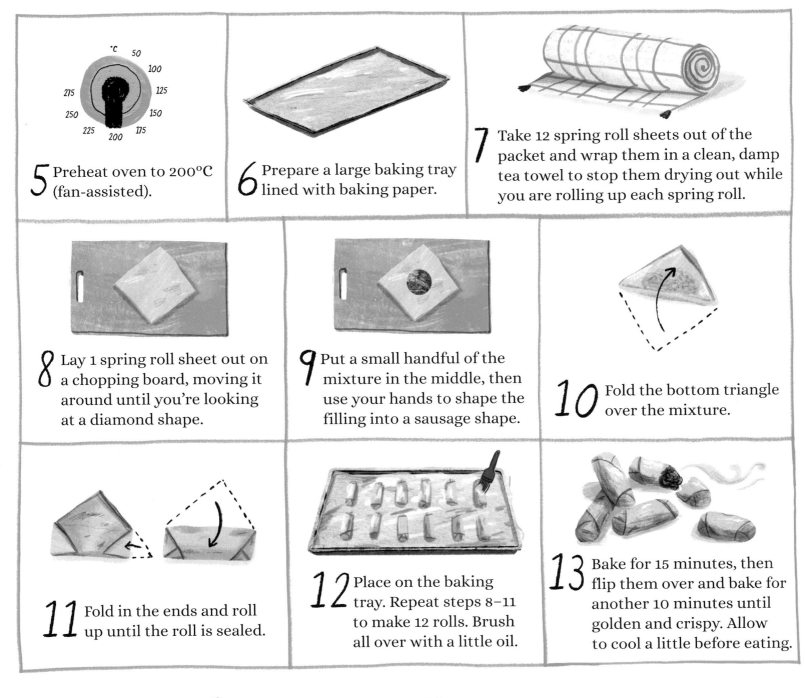

5 Preheat oven to 200°C (fan-assisted).

6 Prepare a large baking tray lined with baking paper.

7 Take 12 spring roll sheets out of the packet and wrap them in a clean, damp tea towel to stop them drying out while you are rolling up each spring roll.

8 Lay 1 spring roll sheet out on a chopping board, moving it around until you're looking at a diamond shape.

9 Put a small handful of the mixture in the middle, then use your hands to shape the filling into a sausage shape.

10 Fold the bottom triangle over the mixture.

11 Fold in the ends and roll up until the roll is sealed.

12 Place on the baking tray. Repeat steps 8–11 to make 12 rolls. Brush all over with a little oil.

13 Bake for 15 minutes, then flip them over and bake for another 10 minutes until golden and crispy. Allow to cool a little before eating.

Snacky samosas

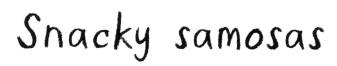

India has some of the best snacky foods, and samosas are my number one! They are crunchy and crisp on the outside and have a soft potato curry on the inside. You can use whatever extra spices you like. I eat these delicious pastries with a fresh salad and a zingy sauce on the side. If you have any filo pastry left over, pop it in the fridge and get it out when you want to make this recipe (or Spring rolls, p.58) again.

Serving suggestion: mix 1 tablespoon of tomato ketchup with 1 tablespoon of mango chutney to make the perfect dipping sauce for your samosas!

Method

Ingredients

2 large King Edward
potatoes (about 350g)

1 small onion

1 small carrot

1 tbsp vegetable oil, plus
extra for brushing

1 tsp garam masala

¼ tsp table salt

30g frozen peas

100g filo pastry

1 tbsp plain flour, for
dusting

≥ Makes 12 samosas ≤

1 Peel the potatoes, chop into 2cm chunks and boil for 10 minutes, until just soft. Drain and set aside to cool.

2 Peel the onion and carrot, then coarsely grate and add to a frying pan with the vegetable oil.

3 Fry on a low/medium heat for 10 minutes, stirring to stop it sticking, then add the garam masala, salt and peas and cook for a further 2 minutes.

4 Pick up the lukewarm potato chunks and crumble into smaller pieces with your fingers. Add them to the frying pan and cook for a further minute. Set aside.

5 Preheat oven to 200°C (fan-assisted).

6 Lay out 1 sheet of filo pastry on a lightly floured surface. Brush the top of the sheet with a little oil, then cut into strips that are about 10–12cm in width.

7 Place 1 heaped dessertspoonful of the potato mixture at one end of the pastry. Gently lift the left-hand corner over the mixture to make a triangle shape.

8 Lift the filled triangle and fold it down to make another triangle shape. Continue lifting and folding, tucking the pastry in tightly.

9 On the last fold, bring the edge of the pastry up to seal the triangle, then brush with a little vegetable oil.

10 Cut out more filo pastry to make 12 samosas. Place them on 2 baking trays lined with baking paper. Brush with a little oil and bake for 10–12 minutes until nicely golden.

11 Allow to cool for 5 minutes, then serve with a crunchy salad and sauce on the side.

Cheese twists

Puff pastry is a tricky technique to master. But don't worry, this is my easy-to-master cheese straw recipe, that takes just a little bit of skill and time. And you won't be disappointed with the final result: delicious crispy twists with melty cheese that are perfect for a treat. You will be very proud you made them yourself.

Ingredients

150g strong white flour, plus extra for dusting

150g plain flour

½ tsp baking powder

200g cold, unsalted butter (diced into 1cm cubes)

140ml cold water

100g Cheddar cheese (grated)

Makes about 20 pastries

Method

1 Put the flours and baking powder into a mixing bowl and toss together. Add the butter cubes.

2 Pour in the cold water, lightly mix with a spatula then gently knead to a dough (try not to squash the butter too much).

3 On a lightly floured surface, roll the dough out to 1cm thick, then fold in half. Wrap and put in the fridge for 30 minutes.

4 Roll the pastry out to about 0.5cm thick. Fold it in half, roll out again to 0.5cm thick, then fold in half again. Wrap and put back in the fridge for 30 minutes.

5 Repeat step 4 one more time.

6 Preheat oven to 180°C (fan-assisted).

7 Line 2 large baking trays with baking paper.

8 On a lightly floured surface, roll the pastry out to 0.5cm thick, then sprinkle the grated cheese onto one half.

9 Fold the pastry over and roll it out again to make a rectangle shape that is about 20cm x 40cm and 0.5cm thick.

10 Cut up to 20 lengths of pastry that are about 2cm wide.

11 Hold each end of the pastry and slowly rotate your hands around and around in opposite directions to gently twist the pastry.

12 Place the pastry twists on the baking trays and carefully press them in place.

13 Bake for 20 minutes until nicely golden and crisp. Allow to cool on a cooling rack before eating.

Sausage roll flowers

Sausage rolls are SO tasty, especially when they're still a little warm out of the oven. I like to make my sausage rolls look really pretty by shaping the pastry into beautiful petals around the filling. It can be tricky to wrap the petals around the sausage meat but, even if they're not perfect, they'll still be delicious, and you'll get better with practice.

Top tip: make the pastries even prettier by adding a squirt of your favourite sauce on top (my favourite is tomato ketchup).

Ingredients

Pastry:

150g strong white flour,
    plus extra for dusting
150g plain flour
½ tsp baking powder
200g cold, unsalted butter
    (diced into 1cm cubes)
120ml cold water

Filling:

3 Cumberland sausages
    (about 150g)

> Makes 8 pastries <

Method

1 Put the flours and baking powder into a mixing bowl and toss through the butter cubes.

2 Pour in the cold water, mix and gently knead to make a dough. Be careful not to squash the butter too much; you want a nice thick layer when it is rolled out.

3 On a lightly floured surface, roll out the pastry to 1cm thick, fold in half, wrap and put in the fridge for 30 minutes (while the dough is chilling, you can chill out too).

4 Roll out the dough to 0.5cm thick. Fold it in half, roll out again to 0.5cm, then fold in half again. Wrap and put back in the fridge for 30 minutes. Repeat this step one more time.

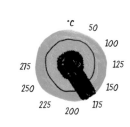

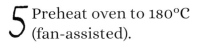

5 Preheat oven to 180°C (fan-assisted).

6 Line a large baking tray with baking paper.

7 Take the pastry out of the fridge and roll it out along the width and length until you have a rectangle shape that is about 20cm x 40cm and 0.5cm thick.

8 Cut out 8 discs with a 10cm cutter, then, using scissors, make 5 snips that are about 7cm long into each disc, leaving a space in the middle. These 5 sections will be your petals.

9 Squeeze the sausage meat out of the skins and break it up into 8 golf-ball-sized pieces.

10 Place 1 piece of sausage meat in the middle of each disc.

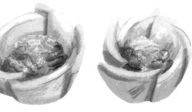

11 Wet your fingers and dab the pastry. Pull one petal up to the sausage ball. Lift the rest of the petals up to the sausage ball, one at a time, so that each petal overlaps the previous one.

12 Repeat until you have 8 pastry flowers, then place them all on the baking tray.

13 Bake for 25 minutes until nicely golden and crisp. Allow to cool on a cooling rack before eating.

Ingredients

Pastry:

50g cold, unsalted butter
(diced into 1cm cubes)

120g plain flour, plus
extra for dusting

30g wholemeal plain flour

1 medium carrot
(about 80g)

1 medium egg

Filling:

1 small carrot

1 small King Edward
potato

100g chicken breast (raw)

½ tsp table salt

2 tbsp barbecue sauce

Makes 4 pasties

BBQ chicken pasties

The most important thing with pasties is making sure you let them cool before tucking in, otherwise you will burn your tongue! These chicken, veggie and barbecue sauce-filled pasties can be eaten fresh or kept in the fridge overnight and eaten the next day while out on an adventure.

Top tip: you can use whatever sauce you like for the filling. I sometimes like to go spicy with a chilli sauce.

1 Rub the butter into the 2 flours with your fingers until the mixture resembles breadcrumbs (or you can blitz the ingredients together in a food processor).

2 Peel and finely grate the carrot and toss through the breadcrumbs.

3 Crack the egg over a little bowl, then gently tip the white and yolk onto your open hand, letting the white fall through your fingers, into the bowl. Set the bowl aside and tip the yolk into the breadcrumb mixture.

4 Knead the mixture for 30 seconds until a dough forms. If the mixture is quite dry, add 1 tsp of cold water to help bring it all together.

5 Wrap and put in the fridge for 30 minutes.

6 Preheat oven to 180°C (fan-assisted).

7 For the filling, peel the carrot and potato, then coarsely grate into a mixing bowl.

8 Add the chicken to a food processor and blitz until minced. Tip into the mixing bowl. Add the salt and sauce, and mix together until everything is combined.

9 Take the dough out of the fridge and divide into 4 pieces. Roll out each piece to make a circle shape that is about 0.5cm thick.

10 Take a quarter of the filling and spoon it onto one half of a pastry circle.

11 Brush the edges with some of the egg white, then fold the empty half over the filled half and press the edges gently together to seal.

12 Fold the edges over again and crimp with a fork, then transfer to a lined baking tray.

13 Brush with egg white and bake for 35 minutes. The filling will be piping hot, so cool for at least 15 minutes before eating.

Ingredients

Pastry:

50g cold, unsalted butter
  (diced into 1cm cubes),
  plus extra for greasing

120g plain flour, plus
  extra for dusting

30g wholemeal plain flour

1 medium carrot (about
  80g, unpeeled)

1 medium egg

Filling:

50g tinned sweetcorn
  (drained)

50g frozen petits pois

5 medium eggs (plus
  leftover egg white from
  the pastry ingredients)

100ml semi-skimmed milk

½ tsp table salt

40g Cheddar cheese
  (grated)

≥ **Makes 12 mini quiches** ≤

Mini quiches

"Quiche" is a French word, but these pretty pastry tarts are now famous all around the world. For this recipe, we use the pastry from my Chicken pasties recipe (p.66) and add an eggy, cheesy filling. These crumbly, delicious and bite-sized quiches are sure to be a family favourite!

Method

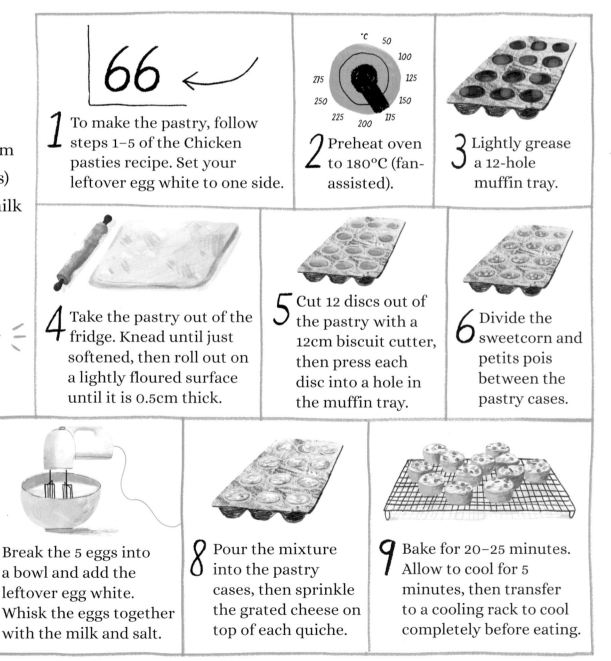

1 To make the pastry, follow steps 1–5 of the Chicken pasties recipe. Set your leftover egg white to one side.

2 Preheat oven to 180°C (fan-assisted).

3 Lightly grease a 12-hole muffin tray.

4 Take the pastry out of the fridge. Knead until just softened, then roll out on a lightly floured surface until it is 0.5cm thick.

5 Cut 12 discs out of the pastry with a 12cm biscuit cutter, then press each disc into a hole in the muffin tray.

6 Divide the sweetcorn and petits pois between the pastry cases.

7 Break the 5 eggs into a bowl and add the leftover egg white. Whisk the eggs together with the milk and salt.

8 Pour the mixture into the pastry cases, then sprinkle the grated cheese on top of each quiche.

9 Bake for 20–25 minutes. Allow to cool for 5 minutes, then transfer to a cooling rack to cool completely before eating.

SHOWSTOPPERS

Ingredients

Bread:

350ml warm water

500g strong white
   bread flour

2 tsp fast-action yeast

1 tsp fine salt, plus
   extra for sprinkling

20ml olive oil, plus
   2 tbsp for greasing

Topping:

1 tbsp olive oil, plus extra
   for brushing

½ green pepper

½ yellow pepper

10 cherry tomatoes

20 currants

4 sprigs of parsley

Makes 10 servings

Focaccia sunflower picture

With this recipe, you can have a go at two jobs: being an artist and a baker! Focaccia is a flat bread, so is a perfect canvas for creating a picture using herbs, fruits and vegetables. I've suggested using peppers, tomatoes, currants and parsley to make a flower picture, but use whatever tasty toppings you like and go with your imagination to make your own picture.

Method

1 In a large mixing bowl, add the water, half of the flour and all of the yeast, then mix with a spatula until it looks like porridge. Cover and leave in a warm place to rise for 1 hour.

2 Add the rest of the flour, salt and oil, then mix with a spatula until a sticky dough forms.

3 Knead and push it around for 3 minutes with the spatula or your hands (do not add flour; it is meant to be sticky).

4 Cover and leave in a warm place to rise for 1 hour.

5 Grease a 30cm x 25cm baking tray with about 2 tablespoons of olive oil. Tip the dough onto the tray and press the dough around with your fingers until it reaches the edges.

6 Brush with 1 tbsp of olive oil, cover and leave to rise for 30 minutes.

7 While the dough is rising, preheat oven to 200°C (fan-assisted).

8 Slice the peppers into small strips and halve the cherry tomatoes.

9 Press your fingers into the dough so that you have about 30 indentations dotted around.

10 Arrange the peppers to look like the petals on a flower and gently press a few currants into the middle of the flower.

11 Make another flower the same way, then add 2 sprigs of parsley for stems and leaves. Finally, lay 2 sprigs across the bottom of the picture and dot tomatoes either side.

12 Bake for 20 minutes, until golden.

13 Once out of the oven, brush with a little more olive oil, sprinkle with salt if you wish, and then leave to cool before slicing and eating.

Ingredients

Cake:

240g unsalted butter
(at room temperature)

420g caster sugar

2 tsp vanilla extract

3 large eggs (at room
temperature)

430g plain flour

3 tsp baking powder

½ tsp table salt

240ml semi-skimmed milk
(at room temperature)

1 tsp red food colour gel

Icing:

100g unsalted butter
(at room temperature)

200g icing sugar

2 tsp vanilla extract

100g cream cheese

1 tsp red food colour gel

Filling:

200g raspberry jam

Makes 12-14 servings

Birthday ombre cake

People will think that you've bought this birthday cake from a fancy bakery. It is iced with different shades of pink buttercream and, if you practise, you'll get better and better at making the icing look neat. This is a BIG cake. You'll need at least 3 mixing bowls and 3 baking tins for this recipe, so make sure you have all of your equipment to hand before you start.

Method

1 Preheat oven to 160°C (fan-assisted).

2 Grease the sides and bottoms of three 20cm round cake tins, and line the bottom of each tin with baking paper.

3 Add the butter and sugar to a large mixing bowl and cream together, using an electric mixer, until light and pale (this may take 5 minutes).

4 Add the vanilla extract, then crack in the eggs one at a time, making sure each one is beaten into the mixture before adding the next.

5 In a medium bowl, toss together the flour, baking powder and salt.

6 Add a third of the flour mixture to the butter mixture and beat until just smooth. Add half the milk, then tip in the rest of the flour mixture, then the remaining milk, beating until smooth each time you add something.

7 Divide the cake mixture into 3 mixing bowls. Put a little food colouring in the first bowl, more in the second and even more in the third. Beat the mixture until each cake batter is a different shade.

8 Divide the mixture equally between the 3 tins and bake for 30–35 minutes, until the cake is just pulling away at the sides of the tin.

9 Allow to cool for 5 minutes, then tip each cake out onto a cooling rack to cool completely.

10 Beat the butter and icing sugar together until smooth. Add the vanilla extract and half the cream cheese and mix. Add the rest of the cream cheese and mix until smooth.

11 Trim the top of each cake to make them flat, then sandwich the cakes together with raspberry jam.

12 Spread half the icing around the sides and top of the cake. You can use a palette knife to smooth it. Set the rest of your icing aside.

13 Put the iced cake in the fridge for at least 20 minutes, until the icing sets.

14 Split the remaining icing into 3 bowls. Put a little bit of food colouring in the first bowl and beat to an even colour. Add a tiny amount to the next bowl and beat. Leave the final bowl without any food colouring.

15 Remove the cake from the fridge, spread the strongest colour icing around the bottom third of the cake, the next colour around the middle, and the rest of the icing around the top third and on top. Try to get it really smooth, then serve.

Ingredients

Pastry:

290g plain flour, plus
   extra for dusting

30g wholemeal plain flour

½ tsp baking powder

100g icing sugar

180g cold, unsalted butter
   (diced into 1cm cubes),
   plus extra for greasing

1 medium egg

1 tsp cold water

Filling:

400g frozen cherries
   (defrosted and drained)

15g cornflour

25ml runny honey

1 tsp vanilla extract

½ tsp almond extract

Topping:

1 tsp caster sugar, for
   sprinkling

≷ Makes 12 servings ≷

Star prize cherry pie

Baking pies can be tricky as the filling is quite wet and can sometimes give the pastry a soggy bottom. To avoid this, you bake the pastry first without the filling, using baking beans (or dried lentils) to hold the pastry in place. I use a star-shaped biscuit cutter to make stars to decorate the pie, but you can also try other shapes. Whatever you decide, this pie recipe is worthy of a star prize!

Method

1 Grease the bottom and sides of a 20cm pie dish and line the base with baking paper.

2 Toss the flours, baking powder and icing sugar in a mixing bowl. Add the diced butter, then rub into the flour mixture until it resembles breadcrumbs.

3 Crack the egg over a small bowl, then gently tip the white and yolk onto your open hand, letting the white fall through your fingers, into the bowl. Set the bowl aside.

4 Add the yolk to the flour mixture with 1 tsp of water. Mix with your hands. When it all starts clumping together, tip it onto a lightly floured surface and squish it with your hands until a dough forms.

5 Wrap and put in the fridge to chill for 30 minutes.

6 Mix the cherries with the cornflour, honey, vanilla and almond extracts and set aside.

7 Preheat oven to 150°C (fan-assisted).

8 On a lightly floured surface, roll out the pastry until you have a large circle that is 0.5cm thick.

9 Lift the pastry over the pie dish and gently press it into the bottom and sides. Cut away the excess pastry, leaving about 0.5cm over the sides of the pie dish.

10 Cover with baking paper, fill with baking beans and bake for 12 minutes. Ask an adult to take it out of the oven and remove the paper with the baking beans. Bake for another 8 minutes.

11 Roll the excess pastry back out. Use a star-shaped biscuit cutter to cut out lots of stars (I use different-sized star cutters).

12 Once the pie crust is out of the oven, trim down the sides (you can eat these extra bits as a treat), add the cherry filling and lay the pastry stars on top, until the filling is covered.

13 Brush with the egg white, sprinkle over the sugar, then bake for 40–45 minutes until golden brown.

Top tip: once you've mastered making this cherry pie, try different fruity fillings.

Ingredients

Meringue:

4 large eggs (at room
   temperature)

250g caster sugar

1 tsp cornflour

1 tsp white malt vinegar
   (or white wine vinegar)

1 tube of red food colour gel

Topping:

1 tsp vanilla extract

200g Greek yogurt

300g strawberries, halved

1 tbsp icing sugar, to dust

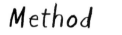
Makes 12 servings

Method

Stripy strawberry pavlova

Once upon a time, someone whisked egg whites and sugar together and made sweet sticky clouds of mixture. They then baked it very slowly and ended up with delicious, crunchy meringue. In Australia, they added cream and fruit on top and called it a pavlova, and now it's a favourite dessert everywhere! For this recipe, you paint lines of food colouring on the inside of a piping bag, so that the light, fluffy mixture comes out all stripy when piped. Beautiful!

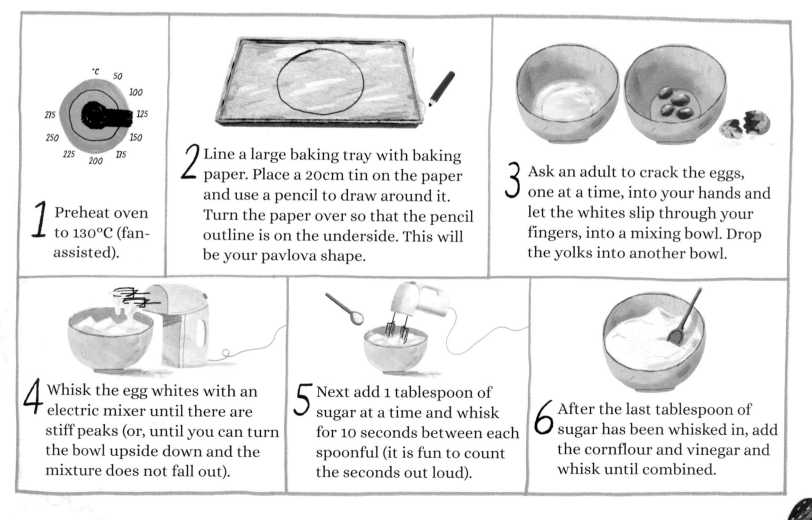

1 Preheat oven to 130°C (fan-assisted).

2 Line a large baking tray with baking paper. Place a 20cm tin on the paper and use a pencil to draw around it. Turn the paper over so that the pencil outline is on the underside. This will be your pavlova shape.

3 Ask an adult to crack the eggs, one at a time, into your hands and let the whites slip through your fingers, into a mixing bowl. Drop the yolks into another bowl.

4 Whisk the egg whites with an electric mixer until there are stiff peaks (or, until you can turn the bowl upside down and the mixture does not fall out).

5 Next add 1 tablespoon of sugar at a time and whisk for 10 seconds between each spoonful (it is fun to count the seconds out loud).

6 After the last tablespoon of sugar has been whisked in, add the cornflour and vinegar and whisk until combined.

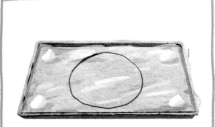

7 Use a little bit of your meringue to stick your baking paper to the baking tray.

8 Ask an adult to hold a piping bag (or sandwich bag) open. Pipe (or paint) lots of vertical, wiggly lines of food colour gel about halfway up the inside of the bag. Use a tablespoon to fill the bag with half the meringue mixture.

9 Spread the other half of the meringue mixture onto the baking paper to fill the circle shape.

10 Cut the end of your piping bag so that you have a 1cm opening, then pipe big swirls all around the edge (but leave a space in the middle).

11 Bake for 1 hour, then switch off the oven and allow to cool in the oven.

12 Take the cool meringue out of the oven. Mix the vanilla extract and yogurt and gently dollop it into the middle. Top with strawberries. Dust with icing sugar, using a sieve, then serve.

David Atherton is the winner of *The Great British Bake Off* 2019. David's cookery books for children, *My First Cook Book: Bake, Make and Learn to Cook* and *My First Green Cook Book: Vegetarian Recipes for Young Cooks* inspired a generation of children to create healthy, imaginative recipes for their friends and family. David is a food writer and an international health adviser for a charity. He has worked on health programmes around the world and never misses an opportunity to explore a new food culture. David is passionate about ensuring that children grow up as food lovers and understand how to make tasty, healthy food.

Harry Woodgate is an award-winning author and illustrator who has worked with clients including Walker Books, National Book Tokens, Andersen Press, *The Sunday Times Magazine*, Harper Collins, Google and Penguin Random House. As well as illustrating *My First Baking Book*, their books include *Grandad's Camper*, *Little Glow*, *The Very Merry Murder Club* and *Timid*. They are passionate about writing and illustrating inclusive books that inspire children to be inquisitive, creative, kind and proud of what makes them unique. As well as illustration, Harry has loved baking from a young age, and dreams of one day owning a bookshop café and artists' space.